COUNTY FERMANAGH

Castle Coole · Florence Court
The Crom Estate

The National Trust

County Fermanagh

'For richness, variety, and softness of shading', wrote the Victorian travel-writer P. Dixon Hardy in 1858, 'we have no hesitation in saying that the scenery of Lough Erne will bear comparison with any other range of landscape.' It is as worthy of such praise today as it was then, with its maze of wooded islands, peninsulas, creeks, loughs, ruins and green hills, even though the area is, unfortunately, threatened by development. The woodlands and wetlands are important habitats for many species and are of enormous conservation value.

The two great houses in Co. Fermanagh which belong to the National Trust – Castle Coole and Florence Court – were built on Plantation estates for families whose rank and fortunes rose during the 18th century. Both are situated in extensive parklands and woodlands which not only provide fine settings for the houses themselves but also support a rich variety of wildlife. Castle Coole, built by James Wyatt, is among the most beautiful Neo-classical country houses in Ireland; its restrained elegance is complemented by sumptuous Regency furnishings supplied by John Preston. Florence Court, set against a backdrop of the Cuilcagh Mountains, is famous for its Rococo plasterwork.

The areas of deciduous woodland on the Crom Estate are rich in birds, rare mosses, lichens, herbs and flowers; the oak woodland is the only known locality in Northern Ireland for the scarce purple hairstreak butterfly, for example; and the damp grasslands are important for breeding waders.

The view from the White Bridge on the Crom Estate

Castle Coole, one of the greatest Neo-classical country houses in Ireland

Detail of plasterwork from the Entrance Hall
at Florence Court, probably dating from the first
phase of decoration of the house, in the 1750s

Castle Coole

Castle Coole possesses none of that 'lived-in' quality so prized by travel-writers and tourists alike. There is little that is intimate or homely about its austere façades and restrained interiors. Yet it possesses an exquisitely awe-inspiring, cold beauty, stemming directly from that austerity and restraint, a beauty which makes it one of the greatest Neo-classical country houses in Ireland and, in the words of James Lees-Milne, 'for sheer abstract beauty the most successful composition of [James Wyatt's] to survive'. The appeal of its severe splendour was summed up by Bougrenet de la Tocnaye, who, shown over the brand-new mansion in 1797 by its proud owner, the 1st Earl of Belmore, agreed that it was 'a superb palace' – yet added that 'temples are fit only for the gods'.

The Entrance Hall and doorway to the main stairs

(*Above*) The entrance front

(*Left*) Detail of the pillars on one of the colonnaded wings which flank the house

5

Armar Lowry-Corry, 1st Earl of Belmore (1740–1802);
pastel portrait by Hugh Douglas Hamilton

James Wyatt (1746–1813), the creator of this 'superb palace', was the most prolific of all 18th-century architects, with more than two hundred projects to his name – and perhaps also the most vilified. His early success, which followed his brilliant Neo-classical designs for the Pantheon in Oxford Street, London, an assembly room which was completed in 1772 when he was only 26, aroused a great deal of professional jealousy, not least from Robert Adam, whom Wyatt supplanted as polite society's favourite architect. His ability to design with equal facility in a range of styles, from Palladian to Greek Revival to Gothic, alienated the purists, and his over-enthusiastic 'restorations' of the cathedrals at Lichfield, Salisbury, Hereford and Ely earned him the enduring nickname of 'Wyatt the Destroyer' as well as the loathing of the 19th-century Gothicists. A.W. Pugin called him 'this monster of architectural depravity – this pest of

James Wyatt (1746–1813); by William Beechey
(Royal Academy, London)

cathedral architecture', and pronounced that 'all that is vile, cunning and rascally is included in the term Wyatt'.

As if such unrestrained condemnation were not enough, Wyatt's total lack of organisational skills and his neglect of his many clients have become legendary. 'Where, infamous beast, where are you? What putrid inn, what stinking tavern or pox-ridden brothel hides your hoary and gluttonous limbs?' stormed William Beckford, infuriated at the architect's delays and evasions during the building of Fonthill Abbey. After his appointment in 1796 as Surveyor-General of the Office of Works he spent so little time at his post that his cleaning-woman was able to run a girls' school in his Whitehall office. And at the time of his death the operations of the Office of Works itself were in such disarray that the whole system had to be reorganised, and the post of Surveyor-General was abolished so that no one man could ever be in such a position of power again.

But in spite of the controversies which surrounded, and still surround, his chaotic professional life (and an equally chaotic personal life, in which drink and women played rather too large a part), during his lifetime Wyatt was acknowledged to be one of the best designers – if not *the* best – of country houses in Great Britain. When Armar Lowry-Corry, then Baron Belmore, decided in the late 1780s to replace his grandfather's Queen Anne house on the Castle Coole Estate with a mansion that would be grander than his brother-in-law's recently remodelled house at Florence Court, Wyatt was the natural choice.

Drawings of the original Queen Anne house which was built by Colonel James Corry in 1709 and destroyed by fire in 1797

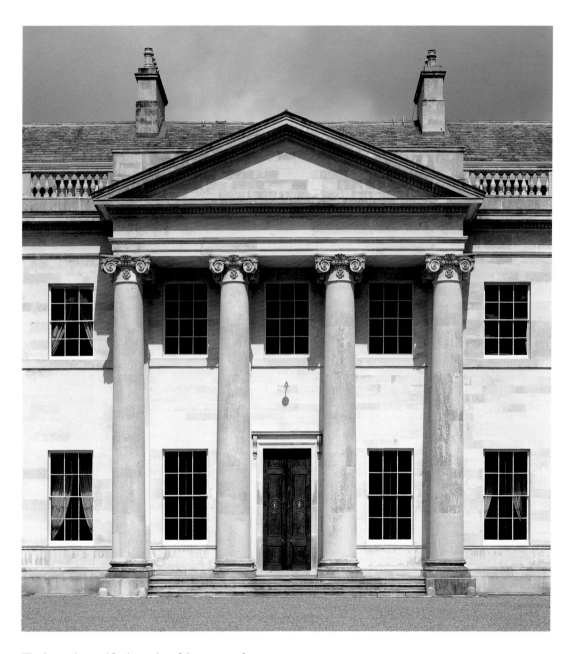

The four-columned Ionic portico of the entrance front

Wyatt was not, however, the first choice: initially Belmore went to the Irish architect Richard Johnston, designer of the assembly rooms in Dublin (now the Gate Theatre) and older brother of the more famous Francis Johnston, whose country houses in both Neo-classical and castellated styles show the influence of Wyatt. The site, half-way up a hill overlooking Lough Coole and the old house, was levelled in 1788, and Johnston's earliest drawings are dated 14 October 1789. But by May of the following year, and probably after work had already begun on the foundations of the house, he had been replaced by Wyatt.

Belmore's decision to employ the much more celebrated Wyatt may well have been connected with the fact that in December 1789 he was created Viscount Belmore: perhaps he felt that his new status required a rather grander, more sophisticated residence than Johnston could provide. Or perhaps he was simply seduced by Wyatt's reputation as the man of the moment.

Wyatt's designs, produced between 1790 and 1793, show a conventional plan not dis-similar to Johnston's original drawings – a fact which adds weight to the idea that work had begun on the building by the time that Wyatt appeared on the scene. But the overall effect is more compact, more concentrated, with fewer details to distract attention from the main composition. Two low, colonnaded wings containing family living accommodation flank a central nine-bay block which houses the state rooms. These consist of an Entrance Hall on the south, approached through a high but shallow portico, and leading into an oval Saloon (which breaks out in a characteristic Wyatt bow on the garden front), with Library, Staircase Hall and Drawing Room on the west, and Breakfast Room, secondary stair and Dining Room to the east. Domestic offices and servants' rooms occupy a basement storey running the full length of the building.

Work began on the construction of the basement in June 1790. As the house took shape, Portland stone for the external cladding was shipped from Dorset to a purpose-built quay at Ballyshannon in Co. Donegal, then brought by barge and cart up Lough Erne to Enniskillen. The west wing, main block and east wing were roofed in 1791, 1792 and 1793 respectively, and the portico was erected in twelve days during June of the next year. Then came the task of fitting out the rooms.

One of a set of mahogany chairs designed by James Wyatt, bearing the Belmore crest, in the Entrance Hall

James Wyatt's design for the rear façade, 1790

Throughout, the architect avoided inflicting the frustrations felt by his other clients at his infrequent and long-delayed site visits by the simple expedient of sending his drawings to Belmore, and not visiting Castle Coole at all. This was a tactic employed not only by Wyatt – who, in spite of a flourishing Irish country-house practice, only ever came to Ireland once – but also in Ireland by Adam and by William Chambers. At Castle Coole, this mail-order approach to country-house building was also followed by several of the fashionable English craftsmen employed by Belmore, including the stuccoist Joseph Rose in London, who was responsible for most of the ceilings in the state rooms. Rose wrote to thank his employer for accepting his cancellation of a proposed site visit:

> I think my Lord I can get some parts of the work modelled in London (under my own inspection), I mean only those parts that are the most difficult – and send them by the wagon to Liverpool and from thence to be

sent to the care of Mr Ellis (in Stafford Street Dublin) to be forwarded to Castle Coole.

And so Lord Belmore's great new house gradually took shape, with Wyatt's designs being implemented – and often altered – either on site by the clerk of works, Alexander Stewart, or back in London where Joseph Rose and the sculptor Richard Westmacott, who carved several of the state-room chimneypieces, were producing many of the decorative details and shipping them off to Ireland. During the summer of 1794 carpenters were at work on the screen of wooden Doric columns in the Entrance Hall, which were then coated in scagliola to represent marble, and on the sash-windows in the Saloon. Chimneypieces and sections of plasterwork were arriving from London and being installed during 1795. By 1797 most of the doorcases had been fitted, the doors and window shutters were hung, and furniture – some bought in, some made on the estate to Wyatt's designs – was appearing.

James Wyatt's proposal for the 'Chimney side of the Library'

The Library at Castle Coole, designed by James Wyatt for the 1st Earl of Belmore and furnished by John Preston for the 2nd Earl

A panel on one of the doors in the Saloon, thought to have been painted by Biagio Rebecca

The screen of Doric columns in the Entrance Hall

However, Lord Belmore was gradually coming to realise that his grand new country house was going to be rather more expensive than he had anticipated. Already by June 1795 the project had cost nearly £54,000, and this excluded Wyatt's fee – usually five per cent of the total estimated cost – and some of the more expensive items, such as Westmacott's chimneypieces. Belmore was torn between a desire for fashionable interiors and a reluctance to pay fashionable prices, and at several points during the building operations he seems to have vacillated between economy and extravagance. For example, in the summer of 1793 he rejected Wyatt's designs for the ceiling of the Staircase Hall as too expensive, and asked Rose to draw up estimates for a plain ceiling without decoration. Rose did as he was told. But then Belmore wrote from Bath, where he was staying at the time, ordering him to draw up a third design, a compromise that was to be neither too plain nor too ornate. This was approved when Belmore called in at Rose's London workshop on his way home – not least, one suspects, because Rose assured him that 'it will not amount to more than half of the first design' – and in March 1795 it was forwarded to Robert Shires, the senior plasterer at Castle Coole.

By 1797 Belmore had moved in to what was, structurally at least, a country house fit for a viscount – fit, indeed, for an earl, which is what he became in November of that year. The perfect proportions of his Entrance Hall promised elegance and splendour. His oval Saloon, with its

elaborate and costly plasterwork by Rose and scagliola pilasters by Domenico Bartoli, was one of the finest in Ireland. His double-return staircase provided a grand ascent to the first floor, with its spectacularly beautiful top-lit Lobby (one of Wyatt's greatest achievements), the Boudoir (now called the Bow Room) and the State Bedroom. But the Drawing Room remained unfinished, and the suite of mahogany furniture which Wyatt had designed remained incomplete. The ornate colour schemes for the interiors were never executed, and the tunnel that had been built to connect the house to a new stable-block led nowhere. In spite of all the compromises, the money had run out.

A stove in the Lobby, installed in 1796

The Bow Room

The Saloon, which was redecorated and furnished by John Preston for the 2nd Earl. The mahogany doors are hung on pivots and curved to conform to the bow of the walls

Somerset Lowry-Corry, 2nd Earl of Belmore (1774–1841); by Hugh Douglas Hamilton

(*Far right*) One of the 'very superb Grecian couches' which John Preston made for the Drawing Room. The couches were so important that they were supplied with two sets of protective covers

Belmore died in 1802, neither the first nor the last nobleman to have built beyond his means. There the story of Castle Coole might have ended had it not been for his son, the 2nd Earl, who, on inheriting what was undoubtedly an architectural masterpiece, resolved to finish and furnish it in the manner that it deserved. New stables were built in 1817, to the designs of Richard Morrison; and between 1807 and 1825 John Preston, one of Dublin's finest upholsterers and interior decorators, was commissioned to redecorate the state rooms. In the Saloon, crimson satin curtains with matching velvet draperies and gold trimmings were installed, and the old furniture – some of it designed by Wyatt, but most probably brought from the early 18th-century house – was replaced by new sofas, stools, tables, lamp-stands and pier-glasses, all in the rather more exuberant Regency taste that was becoming fashionable. The magnificent state bed, described in Preston's accounts as a 'full-sized bed stead ... enriched by carving of very superior design and execution ... [with] a very richly designed tester and dome, with suit of carved and gilt drapery ornaments', arrived in 1821.

In the Drawing Room, Preston's fabrics and trimmings alone came to more than £1,000. (For the journey from Dublin to Enniskillen, the upholsterer supplied 'a very strong dove-tailed chest to contain and preserve the saloon and drawing room and state bed curtains, inside lined with cedar secured with iron hinges with jointed plate and padlock', at a cost of £10 5s.) The room was furnished with what Preston's accounts describe, with a justifiable pride, as 'two very superb Grecian couches ... the entire executed in a very superior style', a set of some thirteen 'very superb armed chairs, seats, backs and arms thickly stuffed and mattressed, French feet and arms richly carved', twelve 'unarmed chairs', and a 'large and singularly beautiful table circular top, broad behul [Boulle] border ... supported by four richly carved and gilt standards upon a shaped porphyry plinth'.

Preston's Regency furnishings are some of the finest in the British Isles; and in the rooms where they predominate, the opulent satins and giltwood complement rather than contrast with Wyatt's stern architecture. But elsewhere – in the sparsely furnished Entrance Hall, or the perfect space of the first-floor Lobby – the interiors of Castle Coole, like its cold façades, still belong to its architect, not 'Wyatt the Destroyer', but Wyatt the creator, even Wyatt the genius.

Castle Coole was transferred to the National Trust by the Ulster Land Fund in 1951. In 1980 the Trust embarked on a major project to restore the stonework at a cost of £3.2 million. The contents are generously loaned by Lord Belmore.

John Preston's magnificent bed-hangings in the State Bedroom; family tradition holds that the State Bedroom was decorated by Preston in anticipation of a possible visit from George IV

Florence Court

Florence Court is something of a mystery. Although it is one of the most important Georgian houses in Ireland, no building records survive, little is known of its architectural development, and its history is a patchwork of conjecture and sometimes contradictory documentary evidence.

What *is* certain is that Florence Court is the creation of three successive generations of the Cole family, powerful Fermanagh landowners whose rise to fame and fortune in the 18th century had its roots, like those of so many of the landed classes in Ulster, in the Plantations of the previous century. Sir John Cole (1680–1726) laid the foundations, both metaphorically and literally, although he died before the house was finished. After a gap of some 30 years his son, the 1st Baron Mount Florence (1709–67), set out to complete in a much more ambitious style what Sir John had begun: he was responsible for the main block. But like his father, he died before the work was complete, and his son, the 1st Earl of Enniskillen (1736–1803), finally brought the project to a conclusion, adding the colonnades and pavilions. The house was extensively restored after a disastrous fire in March 1955.

Florence Cole (*d.*1718), after whom her husband, Sir John Cole, named the house

Relatively little is known of Sir John Cole's Florence Court, save that it owes its name to his wife, Florence Bourchier Wrey of Trebitch in Cornwall. The Cole family had spent the 17th century at Enniskillen Castle, from which, as Governor and Provost, his great-grandfather William had ruled both the town and the surrounding countryside for four decades, until his death in 1653. After the castle was destroyed by fire in 1710 the Coles moved to Portora Castle. But either shortly before Florence Cole's death in 1718, or shortly after, her husband decided to build himself the new country house which was to bear her name. In partnership with Owen Wynne of Hazelwood,

Co. Sligo, he had recently opened up the countryside of south Fermanagh by building a new road from Enniskillen to Sligo. Like the Crichtons at Crom and the Corrys at Castle Coole, Sir John was no longer satisfied with the rigours and inconveniences of life in a fortified tower-house and embarked on a scheme to create a fashionable residence.

In 1739 the Rev. William Henry noted that twenty years previously Sir John had 'cut out noble Vistos, laid out gravell Walks, cut down most of ye Woods ... and in their stead made regular plantations'. One of these 'noble Vistos', a wide avenue shown on an estate map of 1768 and still

Beleek Falls on Lough Erne in the 18th century

discernible in aerial photographs, led straight to the entrance of the present house, suggesting that the Florence Court which stands today was built on the site of, and perhaps even incorporates the basement and foundations of, the earlier house. This was described by the Rev. Henry as 'but small, being only the left wing of a grand building designed by Mr Cole, which he did not live to execute'. However, parts of it must have been habitable, since by the time of his death in 1726 the family were being referred to in documents as 'of Florence Court'. This fact, coupled with the Rev. Henry's remarks, suggests that while the main block of Sir John's house remained incomplete, one at least of the free-standing pavilions which were intended to flank it was in a fit state to be put to use as a dwelling.

For about three decades Sir John's son and heir (another John, who was raised to the peerage as Lord Mount Florence in 1760) apparently had to spend half his life with a half-built house. But in 1754 he received an inheritance, and shortly afterwards began work on transforming Florence Court, sweeping away virtually all of Sir John's house and creating in its stead a much grander and more imposing mansion.

John Cole,
1st Baron Mount Florence
(1709–67)

Enniskillen in the
18th century

The Irish mahogany writing-cabinet in the Library

The main block was probably completed in two phases. The carcase and several of the interiors may have been finished by 1758, the year in which, according to family tradition, a house-warming party was held at Florence Court. The exterior is, in the words of one commentator, endearing rather than fine. The balustraded entrance façade is three storeys high and seven bays wide, the central three bays projecting forward slightly to form a frontispiece. Most of the external decoration is concentrated on this front, and quite a riotous assembly it is – a happy, if unscholarly collection of rusticated corners and window-surrounds, pediments, brackets and keystones. The overall effect is full of dramatic light and shade.

The bold decoration of the Entrance Hall, with its Doric frieze and plaster skulls, phoenixes and masks, probably also belongs to this first phase, as does that of the Library that opens out of it to the north. An Edwardian photograph of the Hall shows the exuberant plasterwork all but concealed behind mounted displays of swords, lances and antlers.

In 1997 family pictures and historic items owned by Captain David Lowry Cole, MBE, the 6th Earl of Enniskillen, were donated to the National Trust as he wished. By doing so, his widow, Nancy, Dowager Countess of Enniskillen, has transformed the house once again to a family home, evocative of centuries of Cole life. The portraits, silver, memorabilia and furniture all have strong associations, not only with the family, but also with local history.

Prior to this extraordinary act of generosity, the Trust had acquired fine examples of Irish furniture, including a mid-18th-century armchair and side-chair. An elegant mahogany writing-cabinet, dating from about 1730, with a swan-necked pediment, inlaid dancing figures and a grotesque mask in the centre of the frieze, is also in the Library. The Countess's Bedroom contains a magnificent Irish 18th-century mahogany bed with elaborate carving, as well as a characteristic side-table with lion mask and deeply carved legs and feet.

The Entrance Hall in 1910

The Entrance Hall today

The next phase of work seems to have begun in about 1762, when Lord Mount Florence, perhaps fired with enthusiasm to celebrate his recently acquired peerage, borrowed £3,000 from a Dublin banker. Two years later, a second house-warming was held – the party that was interrupted, for Abraham Crichton at least, by the burning of Crom Castle (see pp.28–9). The plasterwork of the Dining Room, Drawing Room and Staircase Hall on the west side of the house, and the first-floor chambers, all exhibit a lighter and more sophisticated touch than that of the Entrance Hall, Library and Tea-room, suggesting the introduction of craftsmen from Dublin, as the decoration of his house progressed.

The Drawing Room, which fills the north-west corner of the house, suffered badly in the 1955 fire (see pp.26–7); its elaborate ceiling, the centrepiece of which was a garland surrounding the Cole family crest of a dragon holding a dart, was completely destroyed, and only the frieze survives. The Dining Room was more fortunate; the firefighters had the presence of mind to drill small holes in the ceiling to drain away the water which was being poured into the rooms above, thus preventing it from caving in. Their quick thinking saved some of the best Rococo plasterwork in Ireland. The unknown *stuccadores* provided Lord and Lady Mount Florence with a breathtaking canopy under which to dine, as acanthus foliage swirled round above them, filling and overflowing a

moulded rectangle which has as its centrepiece Zeus, in the form of an eagle surrounded by the Four Winds, brandishing his thunderbolts over the assembled company.

Like the Drawing Room and Dining Room, the decoration of the Inner Hall which separates them is more delicate than that of the rooms on the east front. The cantilevered staircase which fills the Hall rises up past Vitruvian scrolls, large symmetrical panels filled with Rococo ornament and Gothick pendant friezes on both floors. It culminates in a first-floor lobby which is known as the Venetian Room because it is lit by the Venetian window, one of the most attractive features of the entrance façade. Here again vigorous Rococo ornament fills the ceiling and the frieze.

The Dining Room

Detail of the Dining Room ceiling, showing Zeus, in the form of an eagle, and the Four Winds

General Galbraith Lowry Cole

The Drawing Room

Florence Court,
an engraving of 1786
by T. Milton after
I.F. Barralet

While it is tempting to assume that Lord Mount Florence's second house-warming party celebrated the completion of the west range of rooms, this is by no means certain. Work was still continuing on the building in 1767; a codicil added to Lord Mount Florence's will shortly before his death in that year refers to 'Marble Chimney Pieces and cut Stone for the Collonades'.

We do not know whether Mount Florence intended from the first to open out the entrance front into the 80m-long façade that is there today; nor do we know how far advanced the work was at his death. A 1768 estate map of Florence Court shows no evidence of these two wings, but Mount Florence's son William Willoughby (later the 1st Earl of Enniskillen) seems to have completed his father's scheme by about 1771.

Whatever the precise date of the wings, the addition of two flanking pavilions linked to the centre by colonnaded walks – a form made fashionable in Ireland by Richard Castle at Carton (Co. Kildare, 1739) and Russborough (Co. Wicklow, 1741) – has created a much grander impression, while softening some of the eccentricities of the main block. The architect of these wings, which are much more controlled and austere than the central section of the house, may well have been the Sardinian-born Davis Ducart, who was working in Co. Tyrone in the mid-1760s, and who added similar wings to Castletown Cox in Co. Kilkenny in about 1767. Andrew Lambart, the mason in charge of the work (Mount Florence's will also instructs his heir to pay 'Andrew Lambart whatever Sum will remain justly due when the Work is finished'), filled in the space behind the colonnades with a complex of domestic offices and out-buildings, many of which still survive grouped around the Laundry Yard to the south and the Stable Yard to the north.

In the late 1770s, with work on the house finally complete, the 1st Earl commissioned the landscape gardener William King (who also worked at the Countess's family home, Castle Coole) to sweep away the formal gardens which his grandfather had laid out half a century earlier. The avenues and parterres gave place to an uninterrupted expanse of parkland (which by 1834 had been filled with 'many interesting designs of rustic architecture, rockwork, Venetian temple and other erections'); and a five-acre walled garden was created to the north of the house. Originally filled with a mixture of flowers, fruit and vegetables, it has recently been replanted with ornamental flowering trees and roses.

A view from the Summer House across the Pleasure Ground; in the distance is Ben Aughlin

Cane Cottage *c.*1890;
it was built by the 2nd Earl of Enniskillen

John Willoughby Cole,
2nd Earl of Enniskillen
(1768–1840)

William Willoughby Cole,
3rd Earl of Enniskillen
(1807–87)

The house itself changed relatively little after the death of the 1st Earl in 1803, with the exception of the South Pavilion, which was converted into a museum three decades later by his grandson. The 3rd Earl (1807– 87) was an enthusiastic and internationally renowned amateur scientist; he assembled one of the largest collections of fossil fish in the world at Florence Court, comprising some 10,000 specimens. It was sold to the British Museum in 1883, and the South Pavilion subsequently saw service as a billiard room.

The 3rd Earl also made a series of important improvements to the Florence Court Estate. In 1845 he established a tilery and two years later a saw-mill to process timber from what was then a 30,000-acre estate. This water-powered mill and the carpenter's shop to the north of it turned out not only rough timber but also a wide range of products, from cartwheels to coffins.

At the same time, and to the south of the house, the 3rd Earl laid out the Pleasure Ground, a delightful network of winding paths, lawns and ornamental trees and shrubs. From the Pleasure Ground an ice-house, which also dates from the mid-19th century, can be seen on the opposite bank of the river; on the slope above it is a thatched summer-house, recently rebuilt according to old photographs, using the original cobbled floor; and half a mile to the east is the original Florence Court Yew, one of the estate's most famous features. Raised from one of a pair of seedlings found on the slopes of Cuilcagh by a tenant farmer in the 1760s, the tree has an upright rather than a spreading habit. It can only be propagated from cuttings, and so all Irish yews are descended from this one, or its sibling, which the farmer planted in his own garden and which died in the 19th century.

In 1954 Viscount Cole, the only son of the 5th Earl of Enniskillen gave Florence Court to the National Trust. Early on the morning of 22 March 1955 an electrical fault caused a fire to break out on the landing outside the Venetian Room. Although most of the contents were saved – largely through the efforts of the many local people who came to help – by evening, two-thirds of the house had been destroyed. The Trust immediately embarked on a rebuilding programme, with the advice of the architect Sir Albert Richardson. The 5th Earl's nephew, Captain David Lowry Cole, MBE, succeeded as 6th Earl in 1963, and continued to live at Florence Court until 1973, greatly improving the house and estate. The 6th Earl transferred nearly all his Florence Court lands to the Northern Ireland Ministry of Agriculture to make a forest park before his death in 1989. His only son, the 7th Earl, lives in Kenya.

Aerial view of Florence Court taken during the fire of 22 March 1955

The Crom Estate

The ruins of the early 17th-century castle

Like so many Irish country houses, the first family home at the heart of the Crom Estate, which occupies 545 hectares (1,350 acres) on the shores of Upper Lough Erne, was built by a Scottish Planter at the beginning of the 17th century. In 1611 Michael Balfour, the laird of Mountwhinney in Fifeshire, put up a house on the lough opposite Inishfendra Island. Following the usual pattern for a Plantation castle, it was built of lime and stone and enclosed within a bawn some 20m square and 4m high, with flanking towers.

The high stone walls and fortified towers of Balfour's Crom survive today as a picturesque ruin on the shore. In the centre of the main wall of the house there are two towers, one round and the other square, while to the south there are traces of a late 17th-century formal garden and bowling green, enclosed by a battlemented ha-ha. Within this enclosure stand giant yews, said to be the largest in all Ireland.

The reason for the ruinous state of the Old Castle is something of a mystery. Balfour sold Crom in 1619, and by 1655 it had passed to Abraham Crichton, whose family had acquired the neighbouring Plantation estate of Aghalane across the lake in 1613. Crichton, who died in 1705, was colonel of a regiment of horse and foot, fought at the Battle of Aghrim and was twice an MP: first in 1692 for Co. Fermanagh, and then from 1695 to 1699 for Enniskillen. During his time the castle withstood two sieges in the Jacobite Rising of 1689. But according to local tradition, in 1764 its then owner, another Abraham Crichton, was attending a house-warming party at Florence Court when he noticed a glow in the south-eastern skies. Galloping

home, Crichton found that, by a tragic irony, his house had been burned down at the very hour that he was celebrating the completion of Lord Mount Florence's new mansion.

This Abraham Crichton was a considerable landowner and political figure in the area. Born in 1703, he became MP for Lifford, a trustee of the linen manufacture for Munster and Governor of Co. Fermanagh. Four years after the fire, he was raised to the peerage as Baron Erne

of Crom Castle. After his house had been destroyed, he and his second wife Jane (his first, Elizabeth, who had died in 1761, was daughter of John Rogerson, Lord Chief Justice in Ireland) seem to have deserted Crom in favour of Knockballymore House near Clones, which they inherited soon afterwards. Lord Erne died in 1774, and his son John, who was created Earl of Erne in 1789, followed his father's example in spending little time at Crom, preferring to stay in England or to travel on the Continent.

The 1st Earl's eldest son Abraham was declared insane, and as a result the Earl, who died in 1828, left most of his fortune to his eldest grandson, John Crichton. His will stipulated that part of this bequest, £20,000 in Consols, was specifically intended 'to build Crom Castle'; and within the year John had embarked on fulfilling his grandfather's wishes, commissioning designs from the prolific and reliable architect Edward Blore (1787–1879) for a neo-Tudor house built from dark local limestone.

Crom Castle itself does not belong to the National Trust. It is still the property of the 6th Earl of Erne, and is not open to the public. The estate, however, contains a number of attractive and intriguing buildings, many of them not only functional but disposed with an eye to their aesthetic appeal as incidents in a Picturesque landscape. As well as the ruins of Balfour's Old Castle, there is Holy Trinity church, 200m across the lough on the Derryvore peninsula, a Gothic Revival building put up in the early 1840s with a tower added 40 years later in memory of John's wife Selina, Countess of Erne. On the Corlatt peninsula stands a school-house, opened in the 1820s and remodelled in a pretty Tudoresque style in 1848, while a long, low-gabled cottage (once the rectory and now a ruin) stands nearby. Also in 1848 Crichton – by now the 3rd Earl of Erne – erected the Crichton Tower on Gad Island, a little rocky outcrop between Corlatt and the Old Castle. Visible from all over the demesne, the round stone tower had another purpose besides that of eyecatcher: it was used as an observation post for lough races.

Not surprisingly, considering its setting, boats played an important part in the life of Crom in the 19th century. The novelist Shan F. Bullock, who grew up on the estate in the 1870s, remembered Sheridan, 'a gruff, humorous, reddish squat British tar', who was in charge of 'all the fleet, wherries, puts, steamers, yachts, [and] the barge wherein the family [was] rowed sedately to church by two sailors in white tunics and caps'. So perhaps it is fitting that one of the most attractive lakeside buildings is the battlemented Boat House that was put up on the northern shore of Crom opposite Derrybeg in the early 1840s, to the designs

View through the summer-house window

of either Blore or George Sudden. For many years the headquarters of the Lough Erne Yacht Club, the Boat House was closed in 1914; the deaths in the Great War of so many members of the gentry families around the lough (including the then Lord Erne) brought the boat races at Crom to a sad end.

Pleasant though the buildings that decorate the lough at Crom are, their individual contributions are far outweighed by the overall effect. That effect is almost certainly due directly and indirectly to William Sawrey Gilpin, the watercolourist and landscape designer whose uncle, William Gilpin, had been one of the great pioneers of the 18th-century Picturesque movement. Gilpin, whose Irish garden designs include Caledon in Co. Tyrone and Castle Blayney in Co. Monaghan, was commissioned to landscape the demesne in the 1830s; although many of the buildings date from after his death, their positions – carefully placed on peninsulas or islands, or arranged against backdrops of trees or water – respect his definition of romantic scenery, with its 'alternate expectation and discovery'.

Gilpin was probably also responsible for the formal terraces which lie to the south and west of the house, and perhaps for the embellishments that were made to the Old Castle in early Victorian times, the deliberately ruined walls and fake towers. Unfortunately, no papers survive to show us his plans for the estate, no drawings are left to record his designs, and we can only speculate on the precise nature of his contribution to Crom – a sad loss, considering its importance as one of the greatest Picturesque landscapes to survive in Ireland.

Lakeside oak tree on the Crom Estate

(*Left*) A boat moored off the Boat House jetty

A sulphur polypore fungus on a fallen tree in the woodland on Luisherk Island

But Crom is much more than a monument to the past, more even than a refreshing and transcendently beautiful example of nature enhanced – rather than spoiled – by human hand. The historical and aesthetic importance of the Crom Estate is matched by its environmental significance. It is one of the largest areas of semi-natural oak woodland remaining in Ireland, and one of the most important freshwater habitats in the British Isles. The woodlands contain fine stands of oak, probably planted around the time of the 1st Earl of Erne. Other oaks may be as much as four centuries old. Lichens and the diversity of plants and animals suggest that parts of these woodlands may date back to before the New Stone Age, when wildwood covered most of the British Isles.

Such a rich and diverse habitat contains a wide variety of plants, including the wood anemone, violet, wood sedge and wood sanicle. Birds include the wood warbler and garden warbler, and the brimstone butterfly, purple hairstreak and silver-washed fritillary are all in evidence.

Like the woodlands, the shoreline also supports rare plants and animals. White and yellow lilies float on the open water; the dense reed-swamp conceals marsh peas, great crested grebes and sedge warblers. Other marshes contain meadowsweet, yellow iris, purple loosestrife and wild angelica.

By the 1980s Lord Erne feared that the Crom Estate, this rare and precious blend of nature and art, might have to be split up and sold off in lots, its harmony spoiled forever by inappropriate holiday developments and the pressures of late 20th-century recreational tourism. After wide discussions, in March 1987 the estate was acquired by the National Trust, with help and support from Lord Erne, the Department of the Environment and the National Heritage Memorial Fund. The Trust is currently undertaking a major programme of restoration.